TOAST

TOAST

Homage to a Superfood

Nick Parker

PRION

FOR SAM

With special thanks to all the toast-eaters, whose obsessions and enthusiasms were truly inspirational. To everyone who assisted me in writing this book – your support was invaluable. And to the person who suggested Branston Pickle and hummus on toast: that was just inedible.

First published 2002 by
Prion Books Limited
Imperial Works, Perren Street
London NW5 3ED
www.prionbooks.com

Visit www.homagetotoast.co.uk

ISBN 1-85375-483-8

A catalogue record of this book can be obtained from the British Library.

With thanks to Nick Menegatos at the Shepherdess Cafe, London EC1.

Food photography by Jonathan Gregson @ Red Door Management
Food styling by Karen Smith @ Red Door Management
Designed by Grade Design Consultants, London
Printed and bound in China by Everbest Printing Limited

Contents

Introduction

Homage to a superfood

There is a dark secret at the heart of British culinary life. Our kitchen shelves may be bursting with books by Naked Chefs and Domestic Goddesses, but after a hard day at work or a long night in the pub, do we really go home, rummage through our well-stocked larders and knock up a baby spinach salad drizzled with freshly pressed olive oil?

Of course we don't.

We glance briefly into our bare cupboards and then make baked beans on toast. That's if we've got any beans.

And the dark secret is this: we like it this way. No, we *love* it. We may pay lip-service to seared tuna on a bed of rocket but, given the choice, most of us would go for scrambled eggs on a bed of toast any day of the week; if not *every* day of the week. The fact is, we love toast.

'We may pay lip service to seared tuna on a bed of rocket ... but given the choice most of us would go for scrambled egg on a bed of toast any day of the week.'

And yet toast has been shamefully shunned. A veritable casserole of celebrity chefs have been falling over each other in the last few years not only to impart to us the secrets of spatchcocked monkfish with seasonal herb *jus*, but also to impress on us their credentials as 'regular people'[1] by giving us recipes for the 'perfect chip butty' or 'really great sandwiches'. But not one of them has really addressed the food of which we are all most fond: toast.

It's true. I even checked. With a large pile of toast balanced on the arm of the sofa, I studiously dropped crumbs over some of cookery's biggest names: Nigella Lawson's supposedly comprehensive *How to Eat* contains entries on turbot, truffle oil and tataki of tuna, but not toast. Jamie Oliver can offer us gennaro bread (whatever that is), but he doesn't see fit to toast it. A flick through the index of Robert Carrier's *Classic Great Dishes of the World* skips incompletely from *terrine de canard à l'orange* (page 8) to *tomatoes, aioli* (page 78) without a single

---

[1] They aren't. No regular person considers a well-stocked larder to contain anchovies, porcinni mushrooms and polenta. A regular larder can be considered to be well-stocked if it contains even one of the following list: a pint of milk that is still a liquid; bread sans pin mould; some tins, with or without their labels.

reference. Jane Grigson? Toast free. Lynda Brown's *Modern Cook's Manual*? Not a single slice. *The Cambridge World History of Food*, a two volume monster weighing in at over 2000 pages? Not even a crumb. Delia Smith, bless her, does have a genuine entry in her back-to-basics guide *Cooking for Total Morons*, with a brief section on 'how to make toast', but it is really rather elementary, coming as it does between chapters on 'How to tell an egg from a saucepan' and 'What is a carrot?', and so doesn't really count.

This lack of toast literature is not merely a publishing oversight, but a disservice to all of humanity, as everyone knows that toast is not merely grilled bread: toast is one of the finest foodstuffs available to the human race. It is simple, versatile, cheap, utterly delicious and amazingly for something to which so many of us are addicted, it is good for you. Those innocent squares of bread, gently caramelized under a steady heat, are so much more than the sum of their parts. They are the culinary equivalent of those really handy screwdrivers with interchangeable heads. Yet toast has been almost totally ignored. There's even a book about screwdrivers, for goodness' sake.[2]

---

[2] Called *One Good Turn*, by Witold Rybczynski.

I hope this book goes some way to filling the obvious
need for serious treatment of this important subject. What are
the origins of this superfood? Why do we love it so much? What
does this say about us? And what shall we have for
tea tonight?

So pop a couple of slices in the toaster, it's time to pay
homage...

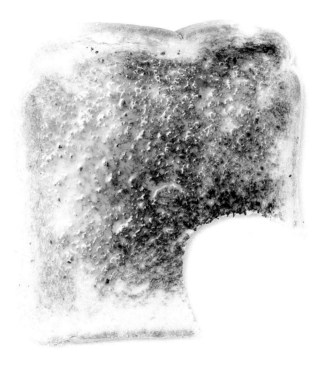

Toast through time

Glimpses of toast in history

In the beginning there was bread

One thing we can be sure of with regard to the history of toast is that the development of bread was pretty much central to its discovery.

The Egyptians made the first leavened breads around 3000 BC. The yeasts in the air from their burgeoning brewing industry settled on their bread doughs, causing them to rise. However, the temperate climate of the Nile Delta, which had made this fermentation so effective, also had a downside: it made their bread go mouldy very quickly. Egyptian bakers found that drying the bread in front of open fires meant that it stayed mould-free much longer. Toasting was born. At least that's one theory.

Another theory is that as the Egyptian brewing industry was growing apace, more and more Egyptians were discovering the joys of rolling home drunk at closing time, stumbling round the kitchen desperate for something to eat and saying 'ssshh' to themselves. Now olives and cheese, while a perfectly fine meal when sober, was not what they wanted after a long night on the beers. With historical hindsight it seems

'One thing we can be sure of with regard to the history of toast is that the **development of bread was pretty much central to its discovery.**'

inevitable that sooner or later some half-cut Nile-dweller accidentally elbowed the family loaf off the kitchen table and into the fire. After much bumbling around, burning his fingers and wrecking the best tea-towel, he pulled the by then perfectly toasted loaf from the flames. And because it is the sort of thing you do when you're drunk, he took a bite, just to see what it was like, and was immeasurably pleased to discover that he had created the first 'munchie' snack.

The Romans were also adept bakers (by 100 BC they had perfected the automatic donkey-powered dough mixer), but they didn't discover toast until they entered Egypt, got drunk on the excellent Egyptian beer and felt peckish. They found another use for toast: it was dry, light and kept for a long time – perfect food for a travelling army. They crammed their rucksacks full of the stuff and headed off to invade Britain.

When the Romans arrived on these shores around 50 BC, our ancestors were mostly still faffing around with unappetising pastes of ground wheat and water, baked into coarse hard lumps and eaten hot (when cold they were too hard and painful to chew). Along with decent roads, civil government,

'**The Romans** didn't discover toast until they entered Egypt, got drunk on the excellent **Egyptian beer** and felt peckish.'

international trade, and a few other minor adjustments, the Romans also popularised leavened bread and toast. Our word 'toast' derives from the Latin *tostum*, meaning to scorch or burn.

There are no records to tell precisely how the Britons came to learn of the Romans' delicious *tostum*; one theory is that they found trails of scorched bread debris behind the marching legions, discarded by the Roman soldiers. The Centurions weren't man enough to eat their crusts.

• • •

It is at the medieval banqueting table that we find another development in the history of toast.

There were no cutlery or plates at medieval tables. Diners served themselves from communal dishes with their fingers, transferring their food onto 'trenchers' – stale squares of flat unleavened bread. By the end of the meal these trenchers were soaked in all the juices and sauces from the various dishes. It is the taste for these soggy bread bases that some historians have cited as a precursor of our fondness for 'things' on toast.

It is sometimes said that we seldom learn lessons from history; well, here's an easy one. If you want to know what it feels like to go to a medieval banquet, don't go to one of those theme restaurants where the waiters dress up in codpieces and they serve your Diet Coke in goblets, stay at home and eat baked beans on toast with your fingers. It'll be more historically authentic and the food will be better.

• • •

The historian H. D. Renner was of the opinion that stale bread was the reason why the British took to toasting in a big way. He said, 'Village life makes stale bread so common that toasting has become a national habit restricted to the British Isles'.

There is certainly some truth in this. In the 16th and 17th centuries rural villagers baked loaves weighing in at nearly 6lb, large enough to keep them going for nearly a fortnight. After the first couple of days these loaves were stale and hard, and toasting was handy for making the following 12 days tolerable breadwise.

'If you want to know what it feels like to be at a **medieval banquet** then eat beans on toast with your hands.'

However, Elizabeth David, the undisputed doyenne of English cookery[1], was unconvinced by Renner's thesis. She pointed out that bread would have been going rock hard all over Europe for centuries and was hardly something that the British had a monopoly over. She is of the opinion that it was the proliferation of open ranges in British dwellings that probably clinched it: by making toasting pretty much anything the natural method of cooking (whereas throughout Europe bubbling pots of broth were the norm, with any leftovers of stale bread being added to the soup as sops).

The good side to quoting Elizabeth David's theory is that there is much culinary kudos to be gained by dropping Elizabeth David's name into foodie conversations, whereas nowadays nobody has the foggiest idea who H. D. Renner was.

• • •

---

[1] Undisputed doyenne she may have been, but she was unfortunately not a great fan of toast herself, admitting that she was 'toast-resistant'. Her celebrated opus *English Bread and Yeast Cookery*, which runs to nearly 600 pages and contains musings on everything from the origin of the bread tin to whether a certain type of victorian bun should be called a 'Wig' or a 'Wigg' contains just five scant pages on toast, and one of these is padded out with an irrelevant drawing of a cottage loaf.

In the 16th century toast started to arouse interest in the homes of the more well-to-do. This produced such delicacies as *pokerounce* – toast with hot honey, spiced with ginger, cinnamon and garlingale – and *toast raille* – toast spread with a paste of sugar and rice flour, topped with a spiced mixture of cooked quince, raisins and nuts, finished with gilt sugar lozenges. Sweet and spicy meat toppings, such as chopped veal mixed with egg yolks, sugar, rosewater, cinnamon and ginger also became fashionable. Butter was not yet used to moisten the toast, instead dabbings of sweet wine were applied.

Meanwhile, the poor cottagers were still toasting their stale chunks of bread and wondering what the hell 'quince' was.

In the 17th and 18th centuries less elaborate toppings became popular, including poached eggs, anchovies, melted cheese and bacon (not all at once). By the 19th century such dishes formed what was known as the 'savoury' course served at the end of formal Victorian dinners. Savouries were designed to clear the palette before passing the port or as a handy excuse for more wine-drinking. Soon people were divorcing these savouries from their seven-course food marathons and eating them on their own. They were particularly handy for using up leftovers.

Meanwhile, the cottagers had still not got their hands on any quinces. And their bread was now often adulterated with chalk or lime to make it appear whiter. They kept eating toast, though.

While savoury toasts were spreading the popularity of 'something' on toast, the establishment of another great British institution – tea drinking – helped to cement buttered toast as a national favourite. Tea drinking had become terribly fashionable among well-to-do ladies in the 18th century, and toast was the most popular accompaniment. Soon everyone was following suit and taking afternoon tea as well as making pots of tea for breakfast and dinner, and accompanying their brew at every available opportunity with toast.

Meanwhile, those cottagers too poor to afford tea sometimes coloured hot water with burnt toast scrapings so that it took on a tea-like tinge.[2]

• • •

---

[2] Life could be really shitty if you were a cottager (in case you hadn't noticed).

To rectify a slur by omission on toast's place in the history books: the sandwich – the snack invented in 1765 by John Montagu, the 4th Earl of Sandwich, supposedly so that he could sustain himself during a non-stop 24 hour gambling binge, and to which he famously gave his name – was actually pieces of salt beef between *two slices of toast*. This can be clearly seen from the origin of the story, as reported in Grosley's *Tour of London*. 'A minister of state passed four and twenty hours at a public gaming-table, so absorpt in play that, during the whole time, he had no subsistence but a bit of beef, between two slices of toasted bread, which he eat without ever quitting the game. This new dish grew highly in vogue, during my residence in London: it was called by the name of the minister who invented it.'

Interestingly, the present Earl of Sandwich runs a high-class catering business, delivering posh sandwiches to corporate clients. If the current Earl wanted to go on a 24-hour gambling binge and suddenly felt the urge for one of his ancestor's bread snack creations, he could have rushed to him on a special sandwich-delivery moped an air-dried ham and asparagus in rosemary focaccia bread sandwich; a crayfish, avocado and chilli jam on ciabatta sandwich; or a flaked duck with hoisin sauce, spring onion and cucumber wrap. Regrettably, none of them is toasted.

Can toast heal the sick?

Toast has a long history as a foodstuff considered to be beneficial to the sick and infirm. Now, unquestionably, toast is a splendid food but whether it really has medicinal properties is another matter entirely. The association probably has something to do with the fact that plain toast is free from strong flavours and unlikely to upset the stomach. The 1945 book *Cooking for the Invalid* thought highly of toast, even stipulating that toast for invalids must be cut into triangles.[3]

Mrs Beeton, usually a paragon of sensible and down-to-earth culinary advice, takes toast for the sick to sublime lengths. In her *Book of Household Management* she recommends that a good food for invalids is a 'toast sandwich', which really does

---

[3] This is perhaps one of the earliest examples of food feng shui. Initially thought to be total bunkum, recent studies have shown that pasta made in the shape of the sanskrit symbol for calm – which is a tube – can aid digestion by up to 43 per cent.

'recent studies have shown

that pasta made in the

shape of the sanskrit

symbol for calm –

which is a tube

– can aid digestion

by up to 43 per cent'

consist of 'a very thin piece of cold toast between 2 slices of thin bread-and-butter, in the form of a sandwich'. This will, she claims, 'be found very tempting to the appetite of an invalid'.

It is just possible that, while in the grip of brain fever or similar excellent sounding 19th century ailment, one might have hallucinated that a toast sandwich was a rich and appetising taste sensation. For those who remained unconvinced, however, Mrs B. conceded that it might be 'flavoured lightly with salt and pepper'.[4]

As though the ever-present danger of being forced to eat a toast sandwich wasn't enough to contend with, being ill in the 19th century also carried with it the distinct possibility of having to drink toast water. Yes, toast water really was a glass of water flavoured with a piece of toast.

---

[4] It is perhaps worth noting that Mrs Beeton's decline as a stalwart of Victorian household management can be traced back to this point in her career. She quickly followed her recipe for the toast sandwich with one for egg omelette, and another suggesting that mashed potato would make a tasty filling for jacket potatoes. From here it was just a short route to her well-documented decline into the opium and mescalin abuse which so marred her final days as a cook.

The principle at work here seems to have been a kind of toast-homeopathy. It was thought that the toast – with all its bready heartiness as the staple food and the staff of life – would infuse the water with its goodness, making a restorative tonic which would help aid recovery from all sorts of ailments, from the common cold to smallpox.

Precisely how best to make toast water was the subject of hot debate amongst cooks and quacks of the 19th century. Mrs Beeton offered a simple method using 'a piece of hard crust' toasted to a 'nice brown': 'Put it into a jug, pour the boiling water over it, cover it closely, and let it remain until cold. When strained, it will be ready for use'. An eminent doctor of the time alleged that the bread charcoal which resulted from burnt toast was an effective purifier, and therefore he recommended that toast should actually be set on fire before being added to the water. The noted Victorian chef, Alexis Soyer, disagreed, drawing the comparison that 'if your house was burnt to ashes, it would be valueless, and the same with burnt bread, which merely makes the water black, and the nutrient of the bread, intended to relieve the chest, has evaporated into smoke by being burnt'.

Unsurprisingly, there is no truth in the belief that toast water is any better for you than drinking a glass of plain water. Not only is it medically worthless, but it also really does taste as foul as you would suspect. If you want to experience this particularly useless and repellent beverage for yourselves, it is worth noting that you needn't bother with all the faffing around with muslin cloth filters and the like – wait till the next time you have had toast for breakfast, and once you have washed up the plates, drink the washing-up water. It'll taste exactly the same.

● ● ●

The coming of the machine

The first toaster was invented in Great Britain in 1893, no doubt prompted by our national devotion to toast. It wasn't until 1919 that an American, Charles Strite, invented the pop-up toaster. Until that time, toasters had to be watched as carefully as toast on an open fire because, unless unplugged, they would keep on toasting until the bread burst into flames.

Nowadays toasters come in all shapes and sizes, some simple, some complex – some will burn the face of Hello Kitty on to your toast, others will burn a comprehensive weather report.[5] Some are old and are now collectors' items, and creepy people on the Internet will pay a lot of money for them. Some are cheap and crap, with pictures of ears of wheat on the sides and nobody will pay 20 pence for them – which is why there are so many at car boot sales.

Toasters are the domestic appliances of which we are most fond. Partly this must be because while our irons, food mixers, microwaves and so on are getting more and more hi-tech, toasters are always destined to remain a bit stupid. We are all so particular about our toast, we'll never fully trust toasters to make it without our constant coaxing and intervening. This makes them seem slow and dim-witted, and makes us protective of them.

• • •

---

[5] Yes, really.

A clever thing your toaster *can* do: make croûtons. Smear a generous, though not too liberal, spoonful of olive oil over a thickish slice of bread, then sprinkle with salt and toast in the usual way. When it pops up – hey presto – you have one enormous crispy croûton, which, obviously, can then be cut into normal-sized croûtons.

A thing that seems clever first of all, but turns out to be downright dangerous: trying to make garlic bread in a toaster. Putting garlic butter on a slice of untoasted bread and popping it into the toaster will almost certainly cause your appliance to burst into flames. You will then have on your hands a combination of burning fat and electrical fire, which is not good. Leaning the toaster on its side, so that it makes a kind of double-sided mini-grill, might just prevent an outright fire, but your toaster will smoke like a stricken oil rig, set off your fire alarm and your entire house will smell of burned garlic for weeks.

• • •

'...leaning your toaster on its side, so that it makes a kind of double-sided mini-grill, might just prevent an outright fire, but it will smoke like a stricken oil rig, set off your fire alarm and your entire house will smell of burned garlic for weeks.'

Apart from toasters, the other way to cook toast in the modern world – given the now complete absence of open fires and toasting forks – is under a grill.

Advantage of grills: they are very handy if making things-on-toast, as you can toast each side separately, to different degrees of brownness, and also grill the toppings.

Disadvantage of grills: you can never tell whether your toast is done or not. Whenever you peek in, hopeful that you might be able to tell whether your toast is on the verge of browning, it always looks orange in the light of the heating element. It is then always slightly frustrating that you have to take the grill pan out just to check how your toast is doing.

Further disadvantage of grills: if using grill from cold, toasting time is roughly the same as for a toaster. However, if you are using a pre-heated grill, toasting time can be as little as 12 seconds with a moment longer resulting in inedible charred cinders.

• • •

A slice of life

Otto Frederick Rohwedder invented the bread slicer. He began working on it in 1912. His first idea was for a device that sliced the bread and then held the slices together with hat pins. This wasn't a success. There are no records to tell us how many casualties his hat-pin-loaf notched up before he decided that the pins were an unacceptable choking hazard.

In 1928 he designed a machine that sliced and wrapped the bread, which both held the sliced loaf together and helped to prevent it from going stale. *Wonder Bread*, which appeared in America in the 1920s was, in the 1930s, the first commercially available sliced loaf. Those new sliced loaves complemented the early electric toasters perfectly.

It's long been rumoured that when Otto saw something he thought was splendid, he would say, 'Why, that's the best thing since I invented sliced bread,' which earned him a reputation of being rather pompous. Whether or not it is true that whenever he proclaimed this, Mrs Otto would bring her husband back down to earth by miming gagging on a hat pin, is another thing which posterity does not record.

• • •

There have been many other noteworthy moments in the history of toast. The invention of canned goods undoubtedly made the option of having 'something' on toast even quicker and easier. There was outright toast propaganda in the 1930s when the Electrical Development Agency promoted 'the electric breakfast' as a way of boosting use of the national grid during quiet times – posters, books and celebrity endorsements urged the nation to get toasting. Bread rationing during the Second World War saw toasting make a comeback as a way of using up stale bread. Even the invention of the Breville sandwich toaster – a kind of torture device used to suffocate innocent slices of bread in a travesty of honest toasting – could not stop toast's rise to the status of superfood.

'The Breville Sandwich toaster: a kind of torture device used to suffocate innocent slices of bread in a travesty of honest toasting.'

Toastology

Slices of toasting life

Nostalgia on toast

Ask anyone over the age of about 65 for one of their fondest childhood memories, and the chances are that after painting some general picture of endless carefree summers and Swallows and Amazons style adventuring (which they are doing just to annoy you) they'll go all misty-eyed and recall making toast in front of an open fire.

The scene will be something like this. It is winter, the night has drawn in, they have stamped snow from their boots by the back door and untangled themselves from their mittens on elastic running through their duffle coat sleeves. In the fireplace, a log fire is blazing, casting a glow of comfort and safety into which they are drawn. Some enormous pot of nourishing broth, made with bits of animal that are now classified as toxic waste, is bubbling away on the stove, but it won't be ready until Father returns from his humble-yet-honest manual trade. So, to tide themselves over until teatime, they take a slice of bread, secure it on the wide flat prongs of a toasting fork (ever-ready on the hearth) and hold the slice to the fire…

They might tell you that, to get it just right, the toasting of bread on a toasting fork is one of those activities that requires a subtle dexterity. Your bread must be fixed securely to the fork, so that you have maximum control over its angle to the flames. You must not puncture straight through the bread. Poor bread fixing can result in you dropping your slice, and you wouldn't have been allowed another, but would have been made to dust off the ashes as best you could and carry on. Hold your slice too near the flames and the bread might blacken or toast too quickly, so that the insides are not quite right … but in any case – they will be going *really* misty eyed by now – you didn't really want the toast to be done quickly, as toasting in front of an open fire was not about making a pile of toast as quickly as possible. This was about toasting *yourself*, about basking in the cosy heat of the fire, turning the day over in your mind as you turned the bread on your fork, and warming yourself through in a glow of security and homeliness.

By now they will be in a state of full-blown nostalgic reverie. You, on the other hand, will be feeling thoroughly wretched, recalling the shallow emptiness of loitering in the kitchen, picking your nose and impatiently waiting for your toaster to pop. Modern life, with all its fast foods and quick-fixes, seems to have lost for ever some of the simpler pleasures of life, you muse. You may even be tempted to try toasting a piece of bread on the gas ring of your hob in a forlorn attempt to inject a little romance back into the everyday. (In practice you will probably find that the bread will end up burned in the centre and uncooked at the edges, and will taste strangely singed, which is exactly how your knuckles will feel after your too-short dining fork has deposited your slice of bread several times right into the flames.[1])

It is at this point that you should look the smugly reminiscing old-timer straight in the eye, remind them of rationing, outside toilets and the impossibility of getting a decent coffee before 1995, and then go off and check your emails.

---

[1] You can tell that I tried this, can't you?

Homage to a superfood

Some reasons why toast is great, and deserving of homage:

'Things' on toast have always provided an excellent way of using up leftovers. Victorian food-writer Colonel A. R. Kenney-Herbert pronounced that 'Savoury toasts ... ought to be favourably regarded by all thrifty housekeepers, insomuch as they afford an easy and pleasant way of working up fragments of good food that might otherwise be wasted.' This is still true today.[2]

Toast is great because it is the only food that one craves when drunk and that *won't* make you feel worse in the morning. Granted, you have no real judgement over the choices you make after several pints of lager or too many glasses of chardonnay, but when you wake up the next day with a pounding head and see that somehow you made yourself a round of toast instead of eating a kebab, you will bless those heavenly slices as you realise how much worse you could be feeling.

---

[2] Unless your leftovers consist of things like half a bag of pre-washed salad and cold take away curry. They don't work quite so well.

'**Drunk Cooking Tip:**
Anything that involves pans
of boiling water will result
in a trip to Accident and
Emergency. Using the oven
will invariably mean
dozing off and accidentally
burning the house down.
Stick to toast: you know it
makes sense.'

Being drunk and making toast is also better than being drunk and making any other type of food, as toasters are dead simple to operate and much more amenable to being handled by those who've had a few.

A word of caution concerning eating toast when drunk – don't put too much Marmite on it. This is a cruel trick to play on your already dehydrating body.

While we're on the subject of Marmite, pay utmost respect to this brown salty goo. It is one of the few foods that, no matter how much you love it, always tastes better the *less* you have. The correct spreading of Marmite is a similar technique to dry-brushing with oil paints and involves getting the merest hint of Marmite on the surface of the toast. Almost no other food, with the possible exception of 'Gentleman's Relish' (highly spiced anchovy paste) works on this principle. It is like a revenge on consumerism in a jar. Even if you think it tastes like poison, you gotta respect it.

Just for the record, though, it doesn't taste like poison. It tastes great.

Anchovy paste, on the other hand, is utterly vile.

Versatility is one of the main reasons why toast is worthy of homage. You can have toast for breakfast, lunch, tea, supper or as a snack in between. You can have it savoury or you can have it sweet. You can have it plain; you can have it with spreads; or you can put things on top of it and make a more substantial meal. You can have a single slice or you can have an enormous teetering tower of the stuff. You can use it in place of bread for making sandwiches. Let's face it, you can use it pretty much any time for just about anything you want. No other foodstuff is this versatile.

Anybody who tries to claim the same versatility for other edible substances is either lying, or a student. Students will eat cereal for every meal of the day. If they have enough milk on it, they can even make it count for all their necessary fluid intake. That isn't versatility, that's just laziness.

Those students who aren't subsisting on cereal are eating a lot of toast. And I mean a lot of toast. It's surprising that you can't now take a degree in 'Toast and Toast-making'. That

would be a splendid idea. This book might make it to the reading list.[3]

But back to our homage: toast is especially great because it takes an already tasty foodstuff – bread – and, through the simple expedient of adding heat, makes it *even tastier*. A single slice of plain toast is tastier than a single slice of plain bread. This is because at 154°C, the sugars and starches in the bread start to caramelise, intensifying their flavour.

Mind you, it is worth noting that at much more than 154°C, the sugars and grain fibres carbonise instead, which can result in a considerable palling of the flavour. In other words, burnt toast doesn't taste so good.

But who am I to judge? My dad loves his toast burnt and always whacks the dial on the toaster right up to maximum. He says he likes the way burnt toast sticks to your teeth. In

---

[3] Course work would include 'The Social Semiotics of Toast in the Work of Charles Dickens'. Toast is a revealing tool in Dickens' work – we learn all we need to know of the insubstantial Mr Twemlow in *Our Mutual Friend* from the description of him 'sitting over his newspaper, and over his dry toast and weak tea...'

fact he says that calling it 'burnt' isn't fair – he prefers to think of it as 'char-grilled'.

Finally, we should pay homage to the fact that toast is the quintessential comfort food. Chocolate may have the fast track to the endorphin centres in your brain, and may indeed be essential for the basic functioning of women who believe themselves to be Bridget Jones, but it gives a cheap high and inevitably makes you feel guilty and a bit sick. Toast, on the other hand, can quickly conjure up reassuring feelings of childhood teas, favourite telly programmes watched while dribbling alphabetti spaghetti down your chin, and visits to grandparents' cosy houses.

• • •

Sulky toast

Bed and breakfast toast is curious stuff. It is cold and lifeless, and looks like it's in a sulk. To divert your attention away from its sorry state, it is always served in a fancy toast rack atop a paper doily. This diversion never works. The proprietors could set fire to their leaflet rack or be dancing naked around their sachets of instant coffee granules (three in every room, next to the broken travel kettle) and you would still spot in an instant that their toast was an indigestible combination of burned and limp, and tasted of old bookmarks.

This is because B&B toast is not made in regular toasters. B&B toast is made in specially modified industrial machines, available only on the guest-house black market or over the Internet from the former Soviet Union. These devices are able to operate at the very limits of science, allowing toast to be cooked using a unique heating process which results in stone-cold food; for the bread to be crisped in such a way that it becomes more limp than if it had been left out in the rain for a fortnight; and making it possible for all breads – white, brown or wholemeal – to emerge a strange and deathly grey colour after toasting.

These special toasters are prohibitively expensive, to the extent that no B&B can afford to replace their *Readers' Digest* magazines from 1974 with any newer journals. They are also extremely difficult to operate, requiring constant attention and adjustment by all the kitchen staff, which is why the rest of the breakfast is always neglected, and your eggs and bacon are crap as well.

• • •

The appliance of science

Why does toast always seem to land butter side down? This is the most frequently expressed example of Murphy's Law – the belief that 'anything that can go wrong, will go wrong'.

But is it really true?[4] The debate had rumbled on in the scientific community for years. Some hypothesised that the

---

[4] I had no idea. I had once managed to calculate in science class that there was enough energy in a single peanut to heat all the homes in the west Midlands for three weeks. Even allowing for the fact that I had used a dry-roasted peanut instead of a plain salted one, this seemed indication enough that I should not trust my own scientific intuition.

'I never had a piece of toast

Particularly long and wide,

But fell upon the sanded floor,

And always on the buttered side.'

James Payn, 1884

aerodynamics of butter were responsible, some said that there was no truth in the theory at all, and that butter landed in accordance with all the usual laws of probability. To prove this in 1991 a group of scientists threw pieces of toast in the air 300 times and noted that the results were exactly 50:50.[5]

The scientist Robert Matthews wasn't convinced. For starters he reasoned that buttered toast is not usually flung in the air at breakfast, it usually falls gently off plates. He had a sneaking suspicion that toast really did land butter side down more often and that if the experiment was repeated under 'breakfast table' conditions, the matter could be settled once and for all.

To cut a scientific paper short, it turns out that he was right. In the year 2000 he arranged for thousands of schoolchildren to push buttered toast off plates and record how the slices landed. Other groups of children had to push toast with sides labelled merely 'A' and 'B' off plates, in order to rule

---

[5] Others pointed out that standing around flinging toast in the air was a highly improbable thing for a group of scientists to be doing in the first place.

out the possibility of spreads being a deciding factor.[6] The results were conclusive: toast landed butter side down 62 per cent of the time. The crucial factor was height – toast starting from the usual position (butter side up) on a plate, falling off a normal-sized table spins so slowly that it doesn't have time to complete a full revolution and so really does land butter side down more often. One would have to be sitting at a table over eight feet high before the toast could free-fall enough to level out the odds.

Hoorah. Case closed. However, there is something we should bear in mind – namely that Murphy's Law does not just apply to buttered toast – it states that '*anything* that can go wrong, will go wrong'. So, if you are doing an experiment which hypothesises the existence of Murphy's Law, then you have to assume that the experiment will go wrong if at all possible. Therefore, the results which seem to show that toast really does land butter side down are almost certainly erroneous. So either Murphy's Law doesn't exist, and toast does land butter

---

[6] A third unlucky group had to perform the control, pushing peanuts off breakfast tables. The peanuts just rolled away.

side down, or Murphy's Law does exist, in which case we are no nearer the truth. If you see what I mean. But then I could be wrong.[7]

• • •

Take-away toast

Consider prawn toast. These small soggy slabs of minced prawns and sesame seeds, plopped onto toast and then deep-fried, have no precedent in China, where they don't much go for bread, let alone toast.

Prawn toast was concocted by a secret cartel of take-away food barons who, using advanced psychological profiling and human experimentation, perfected a foodstuff which appealed perfectly to the British palette circa 1970 (toasty, plus greasy, plus unthreatening novelty, plus stacks neatly inside small tin tray). What makes the prawn toast such a sublime piece of work is that it is also a blasphemy on all that is fine and tasty about good, honest toast.

---

[7] I was about the peanuts.

The prawn toast has now fallen from grace, but the cartel's powers are growing stronger. They have since created chicken tikka masala, which has quickly become the most popular working-class food in the country, and is now what passes for 'traditional fare' in most British pubs, presumably owing to the fact that it is the nearest thing you can make to a pudding that involves chicken.

Fashionable or edible?

'If allowed to stand and become sodden, toast becomes indigestible. From the fire to the table's the thing.'
Cassell's Universal Cookery Book (1894)

The toast rack is an essential piece of equipment for any toast-lover. Toast racks come in all shapes and sizes, from hopelessly kitsch to the elegantly minimalist, and they perform an essential function. If not allowed to 'breathe' after preparation, toast will sweat and your lovingly crafted mountain of slices will quickly be reduced to mush.

Unfortunately, toast racks are terminally uncool. We'd rather eat soggy toast than subject ourselves to such a style holocaust at the breakfast table. Even if eating alone. We know that being fashion-conscious about toast standing upright in a little metal rack so that it stays nice and fresh is absurd, but we also know that it's just a small step from the toast rack to the tea cosy, at which point it's game over.

But we are being foolish; our toast deserves better. Give those lovingly crafted slices of grilled bread the respect they deserve and let them breathe. Your toasting life will be all the richer for it – you will experience the satisfaction of a job well done, of a shallow affectation conquered – and before long you might even begin to take pride in your toast rack, in all its glorious uncoolness. Of course, you might also start wearing Aran cardigans and tartan zip-up bootees, and knit yourself a tea cosy ... but at least your toast will be nice and crispy.

There are other ways around the toast-sweating problem. One is to put your toaster in the middle of the table and make each slice of toast fresh as it is required – this is a great idea for everyone who has a table three feet from an electrical socket.

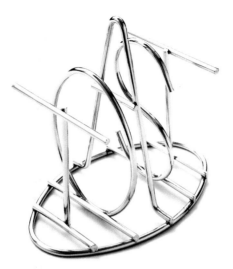

'No matter what novelty

designs are employed, toast

racks will always be naff.'

An alternative is to cunningly stack your toast on the plate so that air can circulate freely around it. Popular stacking shapes are the 'tent' (two slices leaned together at the top edge) and the 'wig-wam' (leaning three or four toast triangles together so that their points meet in the middle), while real afficionados opt for the 'carousel' (a star shape of slices standing on their edge, held in place by a whole round of toast on top holding the structure together.) Of course, all these stacking arrangements have the disadvantage of the fact that once the first slice is removed, the whole structure is likely to collapse.

Plus, if you feel self-conscious about using a toast rack, then there's no way on earth you're going to start doing something as anally retentive and (frankly) freakish as this kind of toast origami.

• • •

What does your toast say about you?

If you want to get under someone's skin and find out what makes them tick, you don't need psychometric testing, you don't need Freudian analysis, or graphology, or those ink-blot tests that look either like a butterfly or a naked woman lying in a pool of blood, you need only ask them how they make their toast.

I admit that this is not immediately obvious. For the last decade or so, Britain has been in the grip of a kind of culinary hysteria. It wasn't so long ago that on national telly Delia Smith had to explain to a doubting nation that chilli con carne was 'like a casserole, but with a bit of a kick', and it was nearly a decade later that fruit juice stopped being considered as a starter by many restaurants. We still feel the shame and humiliation of these dark days of ignorance, and we are so keen to make up lost ground that we talk endlessly about extra virgin olive oil, the correct way to crush garlic, or the precise degree of crunchiness we like in our vegetables. We talk about food so incessantly it's a wonder we've got time to eat.

And yet, when I started to ask people about toast, they were strangely inarticulate. They looked at me blankly. 'Toast? Well, I like it – like – toasted, don't I?' No, I didn't mean ciabatta bread. No, not char-grilled, just toasted. No, not in a skillet or a griddle pan. Just in a toaster. No, not drizzled with *anything*.

'Toast-making is like nose-picking: it's best if you do it yourself.'

Just spread with butter, or perhaps margarine. How do you like it?

And then the penny dropped. And it all came out. A lifetime of unacknowledged toasting preferences, an intimate tapestry of likes and dislikes, do's and don'ts, going straight to the core of who they were as individuals. Don't be surprised if you encounter startlingly accurate descriptions of yourself in what follows.

We might as well start with the butter/margarine debate. There are those for whom it has to be butter and there are others for whom it is always margarine. There are those who reserve butter for special occasions. There are those who try to use butter but find that they always forget to take it out of the fridge, so have to use margarine because the butter is too hard.

Some people microwave their left-in-the-fridge butter in order to try and soften it up. They usually end up having margarine anyway, because they leave the butter in the microwave for a nanosecond too long, until the whole block has turned to liquid from the inside and run away.

There are those who don't microwave the butter, but shave thin slivers off the hard block with a sharp knife, and lay these on the toast in tessellating shapes. This takes a lot of work, a steady hand and a recklessly carefree attitude to one's cholesterol level. Beware of these people.

After arranging the mosaic of thin butter slices on their toast, there are a few who will then flash-grill it in order to melt the butter into the toast. These people are lateral thinkers and will be good in a crisis. Especially any sort of crisis involving butter.

There are those for whom cold slabs of butter would be the worst thing in the world. For them, the butter has to be warm and melted, and absorbed into the toast so that it oozes out over the chin and fingers as they sink their teeth into the slice. These people are sensualists and generally make good lovers. But messy dinner guests.

Some people spread their spreads meticulously to the edges of their toast and find that their toast just doesn't taste right unless this is done. Others 'push their spread around pathetically in the middle of the slice' (as one to-the-edger put it, neatly encapsulating the degree of scorn with which one side saw the other). The to-the-edger spreaders regard the pathetically-in-the-middlers as lazy, unrefined, possibly anti-food and quite probably morally corrupt. The in-the-middlers regard the to-the-edgers as anally retentive control freaks who ought to loosen up more.

Some are very particular about the sort of bread they use for toast: it has to be a good dense bread, granary, wholemeal or similar, with seeds that add an extra nutty dimension to the whole ensemble of toasted flavours, and slices thickly cut by their own fair hand from an unsliced loaf.

Others are happy with cheap sliced loaves.

Do not make the mistake of assuming that those who prefer cheap, sliced, chemically manipulated breads don't care about their toast or are indifferent to good food and have uneducated palettes. You will find that they really do like their toast steamy, sticky and insubstantial.[8]

---

[8] But who am I to judge?

Those who are not fussed about whether their toast is browned evenly, leave the bread in the toaster until it pops up and eat it whatever it looks like. Others have fiendishly complex toasting regimes in order to ensure accurate all-over browning. Bread down for a minute; pop; turn slices through 90 degrees; pop down. Pop up again after 30 seconds and turn slices over. Down again. Back up. Swap slots. Down again. If we weren't aware that toasting is a serious business, we would swear that they were in the grip of an obsessive compulsive disorder.

Some claim that when a slice of toast is cut in half, the top half, containing the rounded end of the loaf, is the tastiest. Others favour the square, firmer-cornered bottom half.

There are those who claim that although both halves have their own distinct characteristics, neither one nor the other is superior, and that it is part of the majesty of toast that you get to eat both pieces. It's a bit like yin and yang, they say. These people are good mediators and will excel in people-facing enterprises.

Mind you, if you told any toast-lover that they would 'excel in a people-facing enterprise' they would rightly tell you to piss off.

Even those who favour the softer, curvier textures of the top often agree that when eating thin or lightly-toasted rounds of bread, the bottom half is easier to handle. This is probably something to do with the inherent strength provided by the alignment of the thicker, squarer-edged crusts. The top half is almost always floppier and more unruly, and when piled with marmalade it will always expose you to the risk of depositing a great orangey glob into your lap.

Almost no-one seems to cut their toast the other way, so that each half contains a bottom corner and a top corner. There is no real explanation for this.

There are those who like their bread thick cut and toasted quickly, so that while crunchy on the outside, the slices retain a warm and soft crumb on the inside. Others go for slower browning, which produces a more thorough, crisper form of toast. From this, it might just be possible to make comparisons between thrill-seekers and more thoughtful types.

Some people deliberately buy really tall bread, so that the top bit sticks out of the toaster to yield a combination of well-toasted and hardly-toasted areas. These people are just weird.

To recap: wholemeal bread – sliced thickly – slowly toasted for a deep crispiness, turned two or three times in a toaster so that it is evenly browned, spread thickly with, say, salted butter that has melted deep into the slice (yet still contains a few substantial globules of unmelted butter on the top) cut in half, bottom end eaten first so that the favourite bit (the roundy top bit) is saved till last … *have you any idea how much all this is saying about you?*

• • •

Lonesome toast

One possible reason why we don't talk much about toast is that it is essentially a solitary food. One often makes it for oneself in the morning for breakfast, when still groggy with sleep; as personal comfort food; or as a late-night snack. One would never make toast for a dinner party, so the question 'How

would you like your toast?' doesn't often crop up in foodie conversations. We know exactly what we look for in a slice of toast, but are never called upon to articulate it. Not like pasta, which is served at 84 per cent of all dinner parties and about which a table of thirty-somethings can witter on for hours, dissecting every last nuance of al-denteness.

If you are regularly made to suffer this kind of interminable droning by a group of foodie friends, invite them all round to dinner and serve them alphabetti spaghetti on toast. That'll shut them up.

● ● ●

Nameless blobs

Those excess bits of margarine – the ones covered with toast-crumbs that you have to put back in the tub because you took too much out in the first place, until the tub becomes one-third full of annoying crumb-encrusted lumps that nobody wants to touch – they don't have a name. They need one.

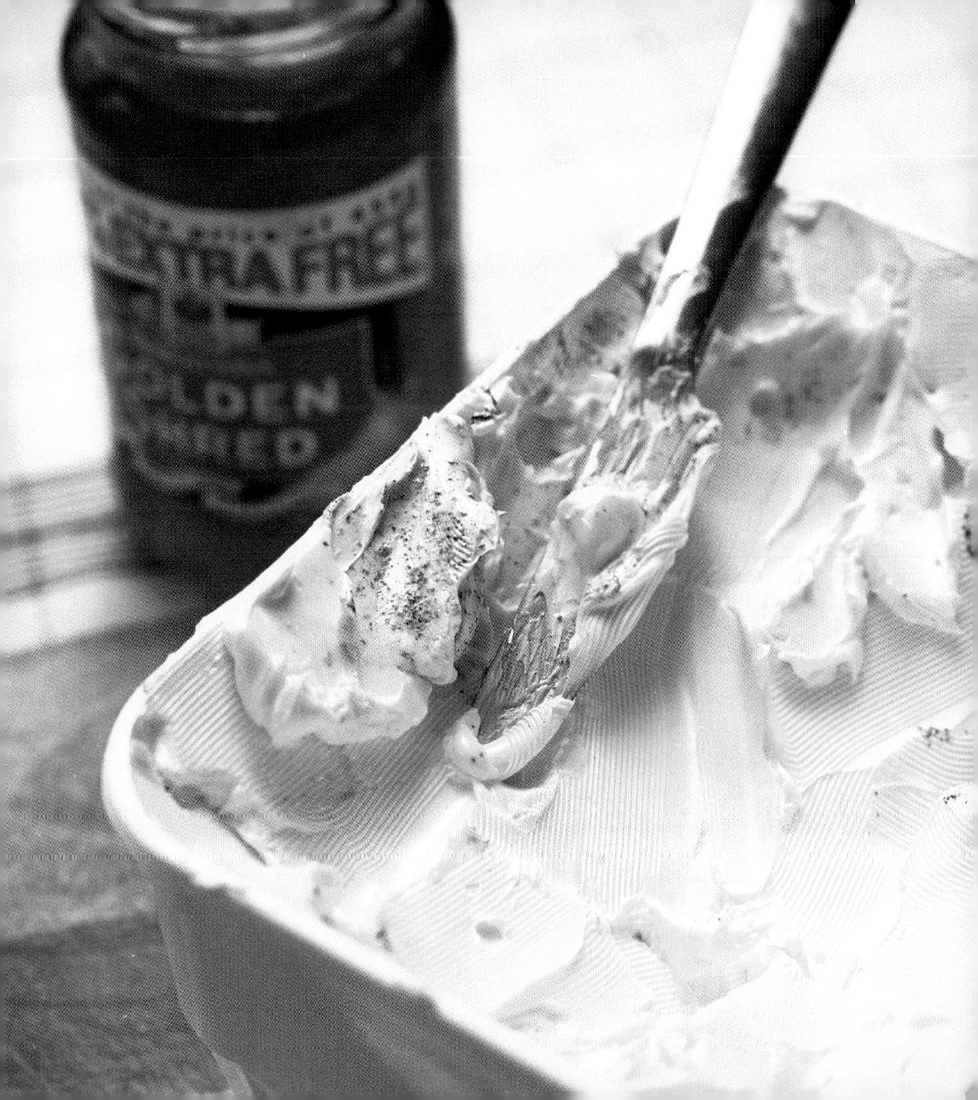

Also: the special kind of amnesia you get when finishing off toast in a toaster for one last time, fully intending to leave it down for a few seconds just to finish it off, but instead you forget about it and wander off and your toast burns to a crisp – there should be a word for that, too.[9]

• • •

Hardcore toast

If you are just a casual toast-eater then you may wish to skip this section and move on to the more light-hearted bit at the end where there are funny jokes about marmalade. If you are serious about your toast, then you will have to confront this at some stage, so you might as well do it now.

There are people out there for whom toppings are a loser's game. They don't mess around with jams, or preserves or curds. They eschew even butter, margarine or low-fat spreads.

---

[9] It could also be used to refer to the mental blackout that happens when you're watching the weather forecast and somehow manage to block out everything that was said about the weather in your region.

They prefer their toast unadulterated.

They eat their toast dry.

At first I admit that it seems unlikely but it's there in all the books. And for the true toast afficionado, it is perhaps an inevitable conclusion: dry toast is toast in its purest form, representing naked confrontation between taste buds and ingredient. Indulgence in toast *for its own sake*, but it's not a foodstuff to be taken lightly. This is the hard stuff.

Be under no illusions, dry toast is *not simply unbuttered toast*. Unbuttered toast is a transitory state, a mere demi-toast, made complete only by the addition of external flavours and textures. Dry toast, by comparison, is the very essence of toast: perfectly crisped throughout, with a toast flavour so rich, deep and poised that it requires no other meddling. Toast *in itself.*

The venerable Mrs Beeton was clearly an indulger, and the hesitant tone she displays in her *Book of Household Management* can give us some clue as to the seriousness of dry toast: '[it] should be more gradually made than buttered toast, as its great beauty consists in its crispness, and this cannot be attained unless the process is slow and the bread is allowed gradually to colour… As soon as each piece is ready, it should be put into a rack, or stood upon its edges, and sent quickly to table.' The recommendation that one should be seen publicly using a toast rack indicates clearly enough what is at stake here.

Others were even sterner. One Sir Henry Thompson, writing at the turn of the 20th century advises us to 'take each piece of toast as soon as it is done, and carefully slice it vertically to produce two half-toasted slices, the untoasted surfaces of which are to be returned to the fire. Such toast will genuinely be crisp, and not scorched on the outside and flabby on the inside'. His method is a little obsessive, but you can't help having a grudging admiration for his devotion to toast.

I have to admit that I was, for a while, drawn into this world of dry-toast eaters. I experienced the euphoric highs of truly well-crisped, dry toast, its meltingly desirable crumb, its deep and penetrating tastiness – but, ultimately, I found I couldn't handle it. For those who may wish to explore further the seldom talked about, nether world of dry toast, with all its toasty rewards, I offer this word of caution: trying to make dry toast in a toaster can drive you to the brink of madness. I will not go into details, suffice to say that, in order to achieve the really thorough crispness that my burgeoning addiction dictated, I had to have the toaster turned to its minimum setting, and to pop, flip and rotate the toast so many times that preparing a simple breakfast took nearly an hour and gave me repetitive strain injury. The concentration involved in trying to cut bread vertically was more than I could cope with early in the morning.

Dry toast is indeed toast for the true connoisseur. Be careful out there.

Toast Recipes

A few crumbs of inspiration

SPECIALS

MUSHROOMS   £1-45

BEANS   £1-25

FRIED EGG   £1-25

Crumbs of Inspiration

There was a time when cookery books were like Bibles. Each household had only one, it contained an answer for everything and reading it aloud would frighten children.

Nowadays we all own hundreds of cookery books by celebrity chefs, all the useful information has been replaced with out-of-focus photographs of novelty vegetables, and just looking at the covers brings on panic attacks of inadequacy. You won't find handy hints for toast-making in celebrity books but if you did, it would be something to do with out-of-focus sea kelp.

Needless to say, there is no sea kelp here. There are not really any recipes, either. But there are a few crumbs of thought about the finer points of toast dishes you've made a thousand times before. If you find one nuance that you've not previously thought of – one more thing to do with Marmite, one new place to stick an egg – I'll consider these recipes a success.[1]

---

[1] If you were hoping for more than just one measly Marmite-related top tip, then I apologise. Take this back and buy a proper cookery book instead.

'Needless to say,

there is no out-of-focus

sea kelp here.'

A word about ingredients

Usually cookery books implore us to find the freshest ingredients available – herbs pulled from the earth as needed, fish and meat still quivering from the final heartbeat, butter so fresh that you can still smell the grass that the cow was grazing on. This does not necessarily apply to matters relating to toast. Sometimes what is required is cheese that comes out of a tube, or a spread with more E's in it than the word 'heebejeebies', making your teeth itch just to look at the jar. So unless absolutely critical, the following recipes don't specify what type of ingredients to use. Experimentation, personal preference and your innate toasty intuition will help you decide whether the situation calls for free-range organic or mechanically processed plastic.

Or more likely, you'll use whatever you've got in the cupboard.

Dry toast

You know the score: for experts and obsessives only. Do not use cheap sliced bread as it contains too much moisture and will steam away to almost nothing. Slice your bread thinly. Toast it *very* slowly and be patient. If using a toaster, turn frequently between short poppings, leaving toast to stand for a few seconds between each plunge. Stand slices in a toast rack when done. Proceed with caution.

Cobbler's toast

Toast only one side of the bread and eat while the untoasted side is still slightly steaming. Butter whichever side takes your fancy. It is not terribly rewarding, has only been included for the sake of thoroughness, and because it is always nice to have a 'proper' name for what is essentially just lazy toasting. So, should you find yourself too lethargic to turn toast over on your grill, or absent mindedly forget to toast the other side, you can pretend that you really wanted 'cobbler's toast' all along.

Buttered toast

Everyone knows how to make this to their own personal specifications, so I return once again to the words of Mrs Beeton, from her *Book of Household Management*, by way of introducing a little cheap historical gravitas into this section:

'A loaf of household bread about two days old answers for making toast better than cottage bread, the latter not being a good shape, and too crusty for the purpose. Cut as many nice even slices as may be required, rather more than a 1/4 inch in thickness, and toast them before a very bright fire, without allowing the bread to blacken, which spoils the appearance and flavour of all toast. When of a nice colour on both sides, put it on a hot plate; divide some good butter into small pieces, place them on the toast, set this before the fire, and when the butter is just beginning to melt, spread it lightly over the toast... It is highly essential to use good butter for making this dish.'

Given that nowadays we rarely have open fires to set our toast before, good buttering can be facilitated by prodding your slice

of toast several times with a fork. This will help the melting butter ooze its way down into the toast.

Crushed black pepper on toast

Make buttered toast according to your preferred method, making sure that your butter is ready warmed, so you can spread it on thickly and it melts deep into the bread. Mill fresh black pepper over the toast and eat while hot. The idea is to get as much of the pepper as possible to stick in the butter, as this reduces the chance of accidentally sucking a piece of crushed peppercorn to the back of your throat and coughing your snack across the room. Unusually for toast, this dish is better accompanied by coffee than tea, as the pepper adds a tingle to the mouth when drinking, which complements coffee well but can make tea taste a bit funny.

Scrambled eggs on toast

This dish has been eaten for centuries, and was originally known as 'buttered eggs', which gives you some idea as to the secret for making a really good batch. Take one egg per round of toast, a dash of milk and a generous blob of butter. As butter has now become one of those things we get hung up about from a death-by-cholesterol perspective, my feeling is that if I told you to add 50g of butter per serving and you thought this was an 'unhealthy' amount, then all you'd taste would be guilt. So use this formula – take as much butter as you can before you think 'ooh, I shouldn't', then add half as much again. If this gives you about 50g per person, then you're on target for a really great batch of scrambled eggs. Don't forget a good pinch of salt and lots of black pepper. Half a teaspoon of English mustard is the real clincher, though.

It is very easy to overcook scrambled eggs and then they are rubbery and take on a metallic taste. As soon as you start to think 'I wonder if these eggs will be done soon?' take them off the heat and the residual heat in the pan will do the rest.

Scrambled eggs are even more versatile than beans when it comes to adding ingredients. Add cooked fresh salmon, flaked haddock, grated cheese, cooked bacon, finely chopped tomatoes or spring onions... If in doubt, it'll probably work.

Mushrooms on toast

About 100-125g of mushrooms will make a generous dollop for one round of toast when cooked. Use wild mushrooms for preference, fresh mushrooms realistically, tinned mushrooms only if your life depends on it. Fry them in a little butter, with plenty of black pepper, and add a small teaspoon of Marmite. Remember to add the Marmite early on, otherwise it won't melt and mix in properly, and you run the risk of swallowing a whole teaspoon of Marmite in one go, which could be fatal.

A small dash of red wine or wine vinegar can also be tasty, but it has to be a very small dash, otherwise your mushrooms will acquire a stale boozy taste, like the smell of pub carpets.

Drain off some of the juice before serving on to toast, unless you are partial to soggy toast.

Cheese on toast

Mature cheeses, bland cheeses, processed cheeses … take your pick. If you generally slice your cheese, then perhaps try grated cheese, and vice versa – you'd be surprised how much this can alter the flavour. If slicing, try not putting the butter on the bread, but spreading on top of the cheese before grilling. Try Branston pickle or mayonnaise or tomato relish or brown sauce under the cheese. A pinch of dried herbs or spices can often change the character of cheese on toast quite dramatically – experiment with oregano or paprika to start with, perhaps moving on to rosemary or cayenne pepper later. Pleasingly, the trendy favourites like saffron and lemongrass will make bugger all difference to cheese on toast.

Cheese and tomato on toast

'Grate some cheddar cheese and spread it on toast. Grill very lightly, then add a half-tomato with a slice of processed cheese on top, and replace under the grill till slightly melted and just browned. (Approx cost 8d)'[2]

This recipe first appeared in *The Guinness Guide to Profitable Snacks*, a work of sublime culinary genius, published in 1961, in order to tell clueless pewter-tankard-clutching publicans (pictured throughout) what food they should flog in their boozers. The masterstroke here is using processed cheese which moulds itself round the tomato half sat in the centre of your toast. Not only is this a clever solution to the problem of getting an even coating of cheese on to the tomato, but it can also make it look amusingly like a boil.

---

[2] The Guide also gives prices for everything. It is a guide to 'profitable snacks' after all.

Posh toast

Nigel Slater calls cheese on toast the 'lazy cook's Welsh rarebit'. I beg to differ. Welsh rarebit is the fussy cook's cheese on toast. If you want a recipe for rarebit, croque monsieur or any other toast dish which attempts to disguise its true origins behind a posh name, then go and look it up somewhere else. Traitor.

Beans on toast

The knack with this dish is not how to make it, but how to get the proportions right when making beans on toast for one person. A normal sized tin of beans (415g) is too large and even if you have three rounds of toast you end up with 'toast *swamped by* beans' as opposed to 'beans *on* toast'; and the half tins (200g) are not enough. If using a full-size tin, giving the beans a quick blast on the highest heat, so boiling off and reducing the juice a little, goes some way to helping (and it's a good way of thickening up the sauce and so intensifying the flavour of economy beans) but does not answer the question fully. Throwing away the beans even before you've started is wasteful and leaves you with a residue of guilt which spoils your meal, but putting a third of a tin of beans in a tuppaware in the fridge is a futile exercise as you just know you'll never use them. Either way, sort out what you are going to do with them before you heat the beans, so you only put the required amount in the pan. Otherwise you'll end up eating them all, destroying the balance of the whole dish and giving yourself 'beany mouth', that tell-tale orange stain at the corners of your mouth, a sign to the world that you just didn't think your beans on toast through properly.

Marmite on toast

As already mentioned, one's relationship with Marmite is almost too personal to admit of comment. Do not allow anyone else to make your Marmite on toast, as you will only be disappointed. Do not get into an argument with an Australian as to which is better, Marmite or Vegimite, as it is completely illogical.[3]

Do, however, add a spoonful of Marmite to just about anything else you ever cook, as it will almost always improve the flavour.

This obviously does not hold true for puddings.

---

[3] Plus, it's obvious – Marmite, of course. Duh.

Pizza toast

Also known as **'poor man's pizza'**. Blob of tomato pasta sauce; grated cheese; Parmesan cheese; any other toppings you have to hand (mushrooms, peppers, olives, things you half remember seeing in Pizza Express); and dried basil or mixed herbs to garnish.

A popular student dish this: toast a thick slice of bread on one side. Spread the pasta sauce on the untoasted side, top with grated cheese and anything else to hand, and grill. Garnish with mixed herbs and a sprinkling of Parmesan cheese. The mixed herbs and Parmesan are important, as it is them that make the psychological difference between thinking about this as a form of pizza and not just as a variation on cheese on toast.

Alternatively, if you are lacking all the ingredients for **Poor Man's Pizza**, then you could try the following:

Poor Man's Poor Man's Pizza

Tomato ketchup, cheese spread and mixed herbs. As above, except with ketchup and cheese spread. Garnish with mixed herbs and use your imagination. If you are lacking all the ingredients for Poor Man's Poor Man's Pizza, then you should seriously consider having something else instead.

The Random Combination

Beans on toast is an undisputed classic. Poor Man's Pizza is an interesting variation on a theme. Hummus and Branston Pickle, however, is a random juxtaposition of two ingredients that were never intended to meet. At this very moment up and down the country people are tucking into all manner of toast dishes which combine foodstuffs in hitherto unimagined ways. Toast's flexibility as a vehicle for such culinary self-expression is to be applauded, as is your inventiveness with salad cream and cold sardines. However, we will not be recording these things for posterity.

Nutella toasts

'Like having a little box of toast chocolates', apparently. Toast and chocolate in glorious harmony. Hallelujah.

Toast bread in the usual manner and spread with a slick of margarine, then, before the marge has fully soaked into the bread, spread with a generous helping of chocolate spread. How much is 'generous'? As much as you can fit on a knife. So use a big knife. It's best to use only one knifeful as, with practice, you will be able to apply the chocolate spread evenly in one swipe, which is helpful as chocolate spread can be difficult to manipulate if you have to add extra. Plus, getting a smooth thick coating of chocolate looks better. Cut each round into a minimum of four pieces – nine for preference, using two diagonal and two horizontal cuts – and pop each piece into the mouth whole as you would a chocolate.

If eaten while still hot, you experience pleasingly squidgy rivers of margarine released from underneath the chocolate spread when you chew.

Peanut butter and 'jelly' on toast

Ingredients: peanut butter and a favourite jam (jelly).

The secret here is achieving the correct balance between the claggy dryness of the peanut butter and the moistness of the jam. Adding butter before the peanut butter helps to oil things a little, but not much. Try peanut butter and jelly in alternate stripes. Try twice as much jam as peanut butter. Using thin toast helps, as maintaining the strength to keep chewing through the peanut butter is quite enough effort, without having to worry about a huge mouthful of dry toast as well. Whether you use crunchy or smooth peanut butter won't make any difference to the sustained chewing marathon you will have to endure – which, in my opinion, makes peanut butter a peculiarly stressful spread for toast.

Cinnamon toast

Popular in England in the 1600s, it went with the Pilgrim Fathers to America, where it thrives as arguably their most popular form of toast. Note that if we can analyse how one's stance on the butter/margarine debate is revealing about one's personality, just imagine what the US preference for sugary-sweet cinammon toast says about the entire American nation.

Mix ground cinammon and brown sugar, using roughly twice as much sugar as cinammon. Make toast, butter generously, and sprinkle with the cinammon mixture, using the butter to 'stick' the sprinkles to the toast. Alternatively, make as for cheese on toast, toasting one side of the bread, buttering the untoasted side, adding the cinammon mixture and then popping the toast under the grill. This is far superior, as grilling caramelizes the brown sugar into a glaze, which adds a whole other flavour dimension.

In Conclusion

We are a nation of toasters. I hope that by sharing Toast's origins, its idiosyncrasies and its recipes, you feel closer to an understanding of toast, and of yourselves.

Toast makes us happy. Toast is growing more and more popular every year. Studies have shown that if we keep toasting at the current rate, we will each be eating 12,000 slices of toast a year by 2007. If our happiness increases in line with our toast consumption, all gloom, despondency and depression will have been eradicated from the globe within ten years – all through the medium of grilled bread.

If this book can help toast bring about global peace and happiness, then that will have been enough.